The Great

Classroom Questions

Plus Comparative Questions

A SCENE BY SCENE TEACHING GUIDE

Amy Farrell

SCENE BY SCENE

ENNISKERRY, IRELAND

Scene by Scene
Enniskerry
Wicklow, Ireland.
www.scenebysceneguides.com

The Great Gatsby Classroom Questions by Amy Farrell.
ISBN 978-1-910949-62-7

Contents

Chapter One

Summary

The speaker introduces himself as a non-judgemental man of privilege, with experience of a wide range of people.

He begins at the end of his story, speaking about Gatsby, who he sees as a man of sensitivity and optimism. He blames those who preyed on Gatsby for being the reason he has closed out interest in the joys and sorrows of men.

The speaker gives some background family information and talks about moving East and working in New York. It is here that his story really begins. He visits his cousin Daisy and her husband, Tom Buchanan, who live across the bay from him, in fashionable East Egg. He joins them and their friend, Miss Baker, for dinner.

The Buchanans live a wealthy, carefree life.

At dinner, Tom talks about a racist book he has been reading and appears convinced by. Daisy, an excellent conversationalist, talks about silly, inconsequential things.

Tom leaves to take a phonecall and is followed shortly afterwards by Daisy.

Miss Baker shushes the narrator so she can eavesdrop on the conversation. She tells Nick (the narrator) that Tom has a woman in New York, a fact she thought everybody knew. Evidently, it is this woman who has telephoned him.

When Tom and Daisy return, the atmosphere is uncomfortable. Later, Daisy tells Nick that she has had a very bad time of things.

Nick chats to Daisy. He feels that her cynicism is insincere and feels uneasy about the evening.

Miss Baker retires for the night. Daisy wants to set her up with Nick. Tom feels she is a nice girl, but says her family give her too much freedom.

As Nick prepares to leave, Tom and Daisy tell him they heard he was engaged to a girl out West, something he says is completely untrue.

Nick returns home and observes Mr. Gatsby star-gazing on his mansion lawn. Nick is about to call to him, but stops himself, thinking the man wants to be alone. He looks away and when he glances back, Gatsby is gone.

Questions

1. What advice did the speaker's father give him when he was younger?
   What does this advice mean?

2. How has this advice impacted on the speaker?

3. "reserving judgements is a matter of infinite hope."
   What does the speaker mean here?

4. What did the speaker want when he came back from the East last autumn?
   What insight does this give you into his character?

5. How does the speaker describe Gatsby as the chapter opens?

6. What do you learn about the speaker's family?

7. Describe the narrator's accommodation in the city.

8. How does the time of year contribute to the story here?

9. What plans does the speaker have?
   What do these plans suggest about him?

10. Describe West Egg, where the speaker lives.

11. Describe Daisy and Tom's lifestyle.
    Does it sound appealing to you?

12. Does the speaker think that Daisy and Tom will settle now that they have come East?
What does this tell you about them?

13. "...on a warm windy evening I drove over to East Egg to see two old friends whom I scarcely knew at all."
Comment on the contradiction here.

14. Describe the Buchanans' house.
What does it tell you about them?

15. Describe Tom Buchanan.
What strikes you about the way the speaker describes him?

16. What are your first impressions of Daisy?

17. Are Tom and Daisy keen to talk about their daughter?
What does this tell you about them?

18. What does Tom say that annoys Nick (the speaker)?
Would this annoy you, in his position?

19. Describe Miss Baker.

20. What is your reaction to Tom's dinner conversation about the white race?
What does this reveal about him?

21. What does Daisy talk about at dinner?
How does this add to your understanding of her character?

22. Daisy calls Nick a rose, something he tells us is not true. Why does she do this?

23. Why does Miss Baker want to eavesdrop on Tom and Daisy?

24. What is your reaction to hearing that Tom has a woman in New York?

25. What is the atmosphere like when Tom and Daisy return to the dinner table?
How would you feel if you were there?

26. What attitude does Daisy have towards her daughter, in your view?

27. What does Daisy's story about her daughter's birth add to the story?

28. How does Daisy make Nick feel that the whole evening has been a trick of some kind?
What is your reaction to this?
How would you feel if you were Nick?

29. Daisy says she will arrange a marriage between Nick and Miss Baker.
What is your response to this?

30. Tom says that Miss Baker is a nice girl whose family ought not to let her run around the country as she does.
What is your response to Tom's view here?

31. What rumour have the Buchanans heard about Nick? How does he respond to their interest in him?

32. What is Mr. Gatsby doing as he stands on the lawn?

33. How is Gatsby presented, as the chapter ends?

34. What are your first impressions of Nick's life and world, based on this opening chapter?

35. What is the appeal of this world?

Chapter Two

Summary

The narrator describes a valley of ashes, overseen by a giant pair of eyes. The trains halt here.

Knowledge of Tom's mistress is widespread. His acquaintances resent Tom turning up with her in popular restaurants.

On the train with Tom one afternoon, Tom insists that they get off by the ashheaps as he wants Nick to meet his girl.

They go to Wilson's garage, where Tom tells Wilson's wife that he wants to meet her.

On the cab ride, Mrs Wilson stops to buy a pup from a vendor.

Nick attempts to part ways, but Tom insists that he come up to the apartment, saying Myrtle's (Mrs Wilson's) feelings will be hurt otherwise.

The speaker says he was drunk on this afternoon in the apartment, which gives everything that happened a hazy cast to it.

Myrtle's sister, Catherine, and a couple called the McKees join the party in the apartment.

Catherine tells Nick that neither Mrs Wilson nor Tom can stand the person they are married to. She says that Tom's wife Daisy is Catholic, and as such, will not have a divorce. Catherine believes this to be what is stopping Tom and Mrs Wilson from being together.

Nick knows that Daisy is not Catholic and is a bit shocked by the lie.

Catherine says that Myrtle was crazy about her husband when she married him, something Myrtle denies.

A second bottle of whiskey is opened. Nick wishes to go, but keeps getting drawn back into conversation.

Mrs Wilson tells Nick she first met Tom on the New York train. As she got into the taxi with him, she told herself that you cannot live forever.

The party is quite confused and fragmented at this stage. Mrs Wilson and Tom argue about Mrs Wilson mentioning Daisy's name and Tom strikes her, breaking her nose.

While Mrs McKee and Catherine fuss over Myrtle, Mr McKee and Nick leave. Nick agrees to have lunch with Mr McKee sometime.

The chapter ends as Nick waits in the train station for the four o'clock train.

Questions

1. Comment on the landscape as Chapter Two begins.
    Does it remind you of anything?
    What is the effect of the eyes of Doctor TJ Eckleburg?

2. Knowledge of Tom's mistress is widespread.
    How do Tom's acquaintances respond to her?
    Why is this, do you think?

3. Where does Tom take Nick to meet his girl?
    What makes him choose this location?

4. Describe Wilson and his wife.

5. Are you surprised that Wilson's wife is Tom's girl?
    Give reasons for your answer.

6. How does Tom view his mistress' husband, Mr Wilson?

7. What does Mrs Wilson want to buy for the apartment?
    What is your response to this?

8. Tom insists that Nick come up to the apartment.
    What does this tell you about him?

9. Describe the apartment.

10. The speaker says that he was drunk on this afternoon in
    the apartment.
    How does this contribute to the atmosphere here?

11.   Describe the party guests.

12.   According to Mrs Wilson's sister, Catherine, neither Mrs Wilson nor Tom can stand the person they are married to.
What is your reaction to this?

13.   What is stopping Mrs Wilson and Tom from being together, according to Catherine?
Is this really the case?
What does this mean?

14.   Is Catherine well-off? Quote to support your answer.

15.   What 'mistake' did Catherine almost make?
What does this reveal about her character?

16.   Myrtle tells her sister that at least she did not marry the man in question.
Describe Myrtle's attitude towards marriage, as you see it.

17.   How did Myrtle and Tom first meet?
Does this sound romantic to you?
What prompted Myrtle to get involved with Tom?
Does this tell you anything about her life?

18.   "People disappeared, reappeared, made plans to go somewhere, and then lost each other, searched for each other, found each other a few feet away."
Describe the final stages of Tom and Myrtle's party.
Does it sound like fun? Why/why not?

19.   Why does Tom strike Mrs Wilson?

        Are you shocked by his behaviour here?

20.   How does the night end for Nick?

21.   Are these characters happy?

        Include examples to support the points you make.

22.   Do these characters enjoy life?

        Include examples to support the points you make.

23.   Would you like to spend time with the characters in this chapter?

        Use examples to support the points you make.

Chapter Three

Summary

There are parties all summer long at Gatsby's.

Nick receives a hand delivered invitation to attend a party at Gatsby's.

He arrives just after seven and is a little ill at ease, surrounded by guests he does not know.

He spots Jordan Baker and greets her. They sit with some other guests. Gatsby is much talked about. The guests do not know him personally, but exchange sensational rumours about him.

They have supper with the group Jordan came with, but they are boring company, so Jordan and Nick go in search of Gatsby.

They come across a man in the library who is amazed and impressed that the books are real.

After some champagne, Nick is enjoying himself. A man recognises him from their time in the war, and invites him out in his hydroplane the next day. This man turns out to be Gatsby.

Gatsby leaves as Chicago is calling him on the wire. Nick is very curious about him.

The guests are in high spirits, enjoying the party.

Gatsby's butler arrives to ask Miss Baker (Jordan) to speak with Gatsby alone.

Many of the remaining women are now arguing with men said to be their husbands.

Jordan Baker and Gatsby exit the library and Jordan tells Nick to call her.

Gatsby reminds Nick that they will take the hydroplane out at nine the next morning.

As he leaves, Nick sees someone has had an accident with their car. He heads home across the lawn.

Nick enjoys the excitement of New York, but he is also aware of the lonely people outside this excitement.

He begins to spend time with Jordan Baker. He recalls the story about her that escaped him at Daisy's. He heard she cheated and moved her golfball from a bad lie in a semi-final. It was almost a scandal, before dying away.

Nick is not bothered by Jordan's dishonesty.

Nick begins to feel that he loves Jordan, so decides to write and break off the vague understanding he has with a girl back home.

Questions

1. What details suggest that the parties at Gatsby's are extravagant?
   Would you like to attend one of Gatsby's parties?
   Why/why not?

2. How was Nick invited to Gatsby's house the first night he went there?
   What would your response be to an invitation like this?

3. Why is Nick ill at ease when he arrives at Gatsby's party?
   How would you feel in his position?

4. Why does Nick decide to attach himself to Jordan Baker?

5. What different rumours does Nick hear about Gatsby?
   How do these rumours contribute to the story?

6. Why do Nick and Jordan leave the group they are with?

7. What is the stout man in the Gothic library surprised by?
   What had he expected?
   What does this tell you about his view of Gatsby?

8. How does Nick meet Gatsby?
   How would you feel, in his position?

9. "Most of the remaining women were now having fights with men said to be their husbands."
   Comment on this line.
   Why are so many of the guests arguing?

What does this suggest about these guests and their
society?

10.   Are you surprised that Gatsby wants to talk to Jordan
        alone?
        What is going on here, do you think?

11.   Overall, does it sound like a good party to you?
        Is there something magical about it?
        Give reasons for your answer.

12.   What details help conjure the party's atmosphere?

13.   Describe Gatsby, based on what you have learned of him
        so far.

14.   What accident occurs fifty feet from Gatsby's door?
        What is going on here?

15.   Describe a typical day for Nick that summer.

16.   Describe Nick's relationship with Jordan Baker.

17.   What story does Nick remember about Jordan?
        What does this tell you about her?

18.   How does Nick feel about Jordan's dishonesty?
        What does this tell you about him?

19.   What does Nick decide to do as the chapter ends?
        What is your response to this?

20.   Nick considers himself to be an honest person.
        Is he honest, in your view?

Chapter Four

Summary

Nick mentions various people that frequented Gatsby's that summer.

One morning in late July, Gatsby arrives to take Nick to lunch. On the drive to town, Gatsby talks about his background, telling Nick that he is from San Francisco and was educated at Oxford. He says that he came into a lot of money when his family died.

Nick is unsure whether Gatsby is telling the truth, but when Gatsby produces a military medal and a photograph of his Oxford days, he is wholly convinced.

Gatsby explains that he wants Nick to know about him as he has a request to ask of him that Jordan will speak to him about. It annoys Nick that Jordan will speak to him about this request on Gatsby's behalf at tea that afternoon.

A motorcycle policeman pulls them over, but promptly leaves when Gatsby produces a Christmas card from the commissioner.

As they cross the Queensboro Bridge, Nick is filled with a sense of possibility.

They join a Mr Wolfsheim for lunch. He recalls the night that Rosy Rosenthal was shot outside the Metropole.

Gatsby apologises for making Nick angry on the way over, before dashing out to make a telephone call.

Wolfsheim speaks highly of Gatsby. On Gatsby's return, he excuses himself and leaves.

Gatsby tells Nick that Wolfsheim is a gambler and that he fixed the World Series in 1919.

Nick spots Tom Buchanan and they go over to say hello. Tom is annoyed that Nick has not called to them for so long. When Nick turns to Gatsby, he has disappeared.

Jordan tells Nick about Gatsby's history with Daisy. She tells him that Daisy was in a relationship with Gatsby in 1917, before she married Tom. Jordan was her bridesmaid. Before the wedding, a drunk Daisy wanted to tell the guests that she had changed her mind. She clutched a letter that she would not let Jordan read.

The following day, Daisy married Tom. Jordan thought that Daisy was mad about him.

Then one night Tom ran into a wagon and the girl with him was mentioned in the papers. The following April, Daisy had their little girl.

Jordan says that Daisy heard of Gatsby again only six weeks ago. She says that Gatsby bought his house to be across the bay from her.

Gatsby wants Nick to invite Daisy to his house so that he can drop by. Gatsby wants her to see his house. Daisy is not to know in advance that Gatsby will be there.

Questions

1. Nick refers to various people that frequented Gatsby's that summer.
   Why does he do this?
   What is the effect of this?

2. Why does Gatsby call to Nick's house?

3. Describe Gatsby's car.
   Does it tell you anything about him?

4. What details about his life does Gatsby reveal to Nick on their drive to town?
   Why does he tell Nick about himself?

5. Does Nick believe all that Gatsby tells him?
   Why/why not? Explain your answer fully.

6. Why is Nick annoyed that Jordan will talk to him about Gatsby at tea that afternoon?
   Do you understand why he feels this way?
   What does this suggest about Nick?

7. How does Gatsby deal with the policeman?
   What does this tell you about Gatsby?

8. How does Nick feel as they cross the Queensboro Bridge?

9. Describe Mr Wolfsheim.

10. What opinion of Gatsby does Wolfsheim have?

11.   Who is Wolfsheim?

            What does this add to the story?

12.   What story about Daisy does Jordan tell Nick?

13.   Why did Daisy ask Jordan to tell the bridal dinner guests that she had changed her mind, in your opinion?

14.   Are you surprised that Daisy went ahead and married Tom?

15.   How did Daisy feel about Tom when they were first married?

            Did Tom feel the same way, do you think?

            Explain your point of view.

16.   What is the significance of Tom running into a wagon one night and it ending up in the papers?

17.   'Gatsby bought that house so that Daisy would be just across the bay.'

            Comment on this line.

            How does it add to the story?

18.   What request does Gatsby make of Nick Carraway?

19.   Why is the location of Gatsby and Daisy's meeting important to him?

            What is your response to this?

20.   What are your impressions of Gatsby now that you know more about him?

Explain your point of view.

21.   Are you surprised that Jordan did not mention anything about Gatsby and Daisy before now?

What is your response to this?

Chapter Five

Summary

Nick returns home and Gatsby crosses the lawn to speak to him. He tells Gatsby that he will invite Daisy to tea.

Gatsby tries to offer Nick some type of work, but Nick says that he is too busy, so Gatsby goes home.

The following day, Nick calls Daisy and invites her over, telling her not to bring Tom.

Gatsby is anxious about seeing Daisy.

Both Gatsby and Daisy are very stiff and formal at first. Gatsby fears that he has made a terrible mistake, but Nick assures him that they are just embarrassed.

Nick leaves the house for half an hour, leaving Gatsby and Daisy by themselves. When he returns, the atmosphere has changed completely. There is a question hanging in the air between Daisy and Gatsby. She has been crying and he is glowing with well-being.

Gatsby invites Nick and Daisy to his house where he shows them around, delighting in Daisy's interest in his home and possessions.

He takes out a pile of shirts and suits and Daisy cries, saying she has never seen such beautiful shirts.

It starts raining, so they do not go to view the grounds, remaining indoors instead. Gatsby calls Mr Klipspringer to play the piano for them.

As Nick says goodbye, he wonders whether Daisy has fallen short of Gatsby's imaginings of her over the last five years. He leaves them talking together, holding hands, and walks out into the rain.

Questions

1. What makes Nick think that his house is on fire?

2. Are you surprised that Gatsby crosses the lawn to speak with him?

3. Is Nick going to help Gatsby with Daisy?
   Would you, in his position?

4. What offer does Gatsby have for Nick?
   Is Nick interested?
   Why is this the case?

5. How do Nick and Gatsby prepare for Daisy's visit?

6. Describe Gatsby's outfit.
   What does his choice of clothing tell you?

7. How does Gatsby behave once Daisy arrives?
   Why is this, do you think?

8. Describe the atmosphere as the meeting commences.

9. Why does Nick go and stand under the tree in the rain?
   What would you do, in his position?

10. Describe the scene when Nick returns to Daisy and Gatsby.

11. Gatsby tells Nick it took him just three years to earn the money to buy his house, but does not tell Nick what

business he is in.
What conclusions do you draw here?

12.   Does Gatsby enjoy showing Daisy around his house?

13.   Why does Daisy cry when Gatsby shows her his shirts?
What is your response to this?

14.   Do you think Gatsby truly cares about Daisy?
Use examples from the text to support the points you
make.

15.   Do you think that Daisy truly cares about Gatsby?
Use examples from the text to support your
view.

16.   How does this encounter between Gatsby and Daisy add
to the story?

17.   As Nick prepares to leave, he sees an expression of
bewilderment on Gatsby's face.
How does he imagine Gatsby is feeling?
How would you feel, if you were Gatsby?

18.   Describe the scene as Nick leaves Daisy and Gatsby.
What is the mood like, at this point in the story?

19.   What, do you think, will happen next?

20.   Are the characters in this novel materialistic?
Refer to the text to support your view.

Chapter Six

Summary

Gatsby's notoriety has spread; one morning a journalist turns up looking for a statement from him.

We learn that Gatsby has humble beginnings as James Gatz. He re-invented himself when he began to work aboard Dan Cody's yacht at the age of seventeen.

When Nick next sees Gatsby, Tom Buchanan has dropped in while out horseriding. Gatsby is rattled by Tom's presence, but when the woman in Tom's party invites him to supper, he wants to go to see more of Tom.

However, the horseriders do not wait for Gatsby and leave without him.

Tom accompanies Daisy to Gatsby's party the following Saturday. Nick finds that his presence brings an air of oppressiveness to the gathering.

Gatsby introduces Tom and Daisy to all of the celebrities in attendance.

Nick sits at a tipsy table for supper, where the guests argue with one another.

As Tom and Daisy wait for their car, Tom wonders who Gatsby is. He intends to discover the man's background and business.

At the party's close, Gatsby is tense and upset because he feels that Daisy did not have a good time.

Gatsby wants Daisy to tell Tom that she never loved him. Then he and Daisy will go and be married from her house. He wants to re-capture the past and insists it can be done. He remembers a magical night walking with Daisy five years previously.

Nick almost replies to him, but cannot find what he was about to say.

Questions

1. Why does a young reporter turn up at Gatsby's door one morning?
    What does this suggest?

2. Who is James Gatz?
    What is your response to this development?

3. What was life like for Gatsby at seventeen?
    Does this surprise you?

4. Who was Dan Cody?

5. Describe the relationship between Gatsby and Dan Cody.

6. What did Gatsby inherit when Dan Cody died?

7. Why doesn't Nick see or speak to Gatsby for several weeks?
    What does this suggest about his relationship with Jordan Baker?

8. Why does Gatsby want to go to supper with Tom Buchanan's party?

9. What does Tom's presence bring to Gatsby's party the following Saturday night?
    Why is this the case, do you think?

10. Why does Gatsby introduce Daisy and Tom to the celebrities at his party, in your view?

11. Describe Tom and Daisy's relationship at this point.

12. Why does Nick feel that he chose a bad table for supper?

13. Why is Daisy appalled by West Egg?

14. What does Tom want to know about Gatsby?

15. Why is Gatsby unhappy when the party ends?
    Does this tell you anything about him?

16. What does Gatsby want from Daisy?
    What is your reaction to this?
    Do you think that Gatsby and Daisy would be happy together?
    Explain your opinion here fully.

17. Comment on Gatsby's recollection from five years ago.
    What does it tell you about Gatsby and his outlook towards life and love?

18. Nick does not speak as the chapter ends. Why not?
    What does this add to the story?

19. What is the mood like as this chapter ends?

20. What possible sources of conflict lie ahead for the characters?
    What outcomes do you imagine?
    Give reasons for your answer.

Chapter Seven

Summary

Gatsby fails to hold a party one Saturday and fires and replaces his staff. He does not want gossip about Daisy, who calls over quite often in the afternoons.

He invites Nick to lunch at Daisy's the next day. Nick thinks that something is up.

It is very hot, the hottest day of the summer. When Nick and Gatsby join Daisy and Jordan, Tom is out in the hall, on the telephone to his girl. The others overhear him talking about not selling his car.

When Tom leaves the room for drinks, Daisy kisses Gatsby on the mouth.

Daisy's daughter is briefly brought in by her nurse to meet the guests.

Daisy complains about the heat during luncheon and wants to go to town. She tells Gatsby that he always looks cool and Tom realises that Daisy loves him.

Angered, Tom agrees to go to town and the women get ready while the men wait.

Gatsby feels he cannot say anything about the affair with Daisy while in Tom's house.

Gatsby offers to drive them to town, but Tom asks to drive Gatsby's car while Gatsby takes Tom's coupé. Daisy chooses to travel with Gatsby, while Nick and Jordan go with Tom. In the car, Tom remarks about Daisy and Gatsby and says he has been investigating him.

They stop for gas at Wilson's garage. Wilson wants to make money selling Tom's car so he and his wife can move out West.

Nick realises Myrtle is watching them. He sees she is jealous when she looks at Jordan, who she assumes is Tom's wife.

Driving on, Tom realises that he is in danger of losing both his wife and his mistress.

They engage the parlour of a suite in the Plaza Hotel, knowing that it is a crazy idea. There is tension in the room.

The wedding downstairs reminds them of Daisy and Tom's wedding. They talk about a guest called Biloxi and realise that he pretended to know them in order to attend.

Tom quizzes Gatsby on his Oxford background. Gatsby says he only attended for five months, after the Armistice, and Nick's faith in him is renewed.

Tom asks Gatsby what kind of a row he is trying to cause in his house.

Gatsby tells Tom that Daisy does not and has not ever loved him. He says that she loves him, Gatsby, instead.

Tom does not believe Gatsby, saying that Daisy does indeed love him, and he her.

At Gatsby's prompting, Daisy tells Tom that she never loved him. Tom then mentions specific occasions and she says that she cannot help the past, that she loved them both.

Gatsby is greatly affected to hear that Daisy loved Tom. Tom vows he will take better care of her in future, but Gatsby insists that she is leaving him, despite Tom's disbelief.

Tom says he knows Gatsby is involved in bootlegging and more.

Gatsby is rattled and tries to defend himself to Daisy, but she draws into herself, away from him.

She asks to leave and Tom tells her to go ahead in Gatsby's car. He is not threatened by Gatsby, the flirtation between him and Daisy is over.

Nick realises it is his thirtieth birthday.

Wilson has been keeping Myrtle locked upstairs. They have a big row and she runs outside and is knocked down and killed.

When Tom sees the wreck, he stops the car to take a look. Myrtle's body is on a work-table in the garage. A policeman takes notes while Wilson wails.

A witness tells the policeman that a yellow car knocked Myrtle down.

Wilson knows Tom was driving this (Gatsby's) car earlier, but witnesses confirm that Tom has come from New York in his coupé.

On the way home, Tom cries and calls Gatsby a coward.

When they reach the Buchanans', Nick does not go in, waiting outside for his taxi. He meets Gatsby, who tells him that Daisy was driving and hit Myrtle Wilson.

Gatsby is waiting outside to make sure that Tom does not bother Daisy. She will signal to Gatsby if he does. He is prepared to wait all night if necessary.

Fearing a commotion if Tom learns that Daisy was driving, Nick returns to the Buchanans'. He looks through the pantry window and sees the couple sitting together, talking.

Nick leaves Gatsby to his unnecessary vigil and goes home.

Questions

1. What has changed at Gatsby's?
   What is going on?

2. Why has Gatsby phoned Nick Carraway?
   Describe the atmosphere at this point.

3. What effect does the extreme heat have on the characters?

4. What is Tom doing when Nick and Gatsby arrive?
   Comment on his actions here.

5. When Tom leaves the room, Daisy kisses Gatsby.
   Why does she do this, do you think?
   What do her actions here suggest about her marriage?

6. Daisy brings her daughter in to show her off to the guests.
   Does she care about her daughter, in your view?
   Is Daisy a good mother? Explain your point of view.

7. How does Daisy act during luncheon?

8. What makes Tom realise that Daisy loves Gatsby?
   How does Tom react once he realises what is going on?
   What makes him react this way?

9. 'I can't say anything in his house, old sport.'
   What stops Gatsby from speaking openly here?

10. Throughout the story, Nick has referred to the wonderful
    quality of Daisy's voice. Here, Gatsby describes her voice

as being full of money.

Are you surprised by his comment?

Is it apt, do you think?

11. Daisy chooses to travel to town with Gatsby in the coupé.

Why does she do this?

Are you surprised by her actions here?

12. Why is Jordan cross with Tom on the drive to town?

What does this tell you about her?

13. Why does Wilson need money?

What does this mean for Tom?

14. In what way is Tom like Wilson, according to Nick?

15. What assumption does Myrtle Wilson make about Jordan?

Why does she feel so strongly about her?

16. What makes Tom feel "the hot whips of panic"?

Do you feel sorry for him?

17. What builds tension in the hotel suite?

18. How does the anecdote about Biloxi add to this scene?

19. What re-affirms Nick's faith in Gatsby?

20. Does Nick have any sympathy for Tom?

Do you? Explain what makes you feel this way about him.

21.   What does Gatsby tell Tom?
      Why, do you think, is it so important to Gatsby to tell
      him this?

22.   How does Tom react to Gatsby's revelation?

23.   How does Gatsby react to hearing that Daisy loved Tom?
      Can you explain his reaction?

24.   Why is Tom not upset to learn that he has a love rival?

25.   Does Tom believe that Daisy will leave him?

26.   What information does Tom reveal about Gatsby?
      Does this surprise you?

27.   How does Daisy react to Tom's accusations?

28.   Tom tells Daisy to travel home with Gatsby.
      What do his instructions here tell you about this situation
      and his personality?

29.   How does Nick feel about turning thirty?

30.   Why did Michaelis, Wilson's neighbour, hear a violent
      racket above the garage?
      What is your response to this?

31.   What has happened to Myrtle Wilson?
      Is this an exciting development in the story?
      Explain your point of view.

32.   How does her husband react to Myrtle's death?

33. Based on the information the witnesses provide, what do you think has happened here?

34. Why is Tom upset as he drives towards home?

35. What does this display of emotion tell you about Tom?

36. Why doesn't Nick want to go in to Tom's house?

37. How does Nick feel about Gatsby as they talk on the driveway?
    Can you explain his emotions here?

38. How did the accident happen, according to Gatsby?

39. How does Gatsby intend to spend the night?
    What is your response to this?

40. Why does Nick go back to the Buchanans'?

41. What does he see through the pantry window?
    Does this surprise you?

42. Do you feel sorry for Gatsby as this chapter ends?
    Give reasons for your answer.

43. Do you feel sorry for Daisy or Tom?
    Clearly explain your point of view.

44. Do you think it is likely that Daisy will leave Tom for Gatsby?
    Explain your point of view.

45.   What is the mood like as this chapter ends?

46.   How does the author make use of conflict and tension in this chapter?

Chapter Eight

Summary

Nick cannot sleep and goes to Gatsby towards dawn.

Nothing happened with Daisy, so Gatsby came home. His house seems enormous and unfamiliar to Nick.

Nick advises Gatsby to leave town, but knows that he won't leave Daisy now. Gatsby tells Nick about Dan Cody and his past with Daisy. He talks about the excitement and mystery that Daisy and her home held for him.

Gatsby let Daisy believe that he was from the same social strata as her. He slept with her one October night and felt committed to her thereafter.

Gatsby rose through the ranks in the army, but was keen to get home to Daisy.

During Gatsby's absence, Daisy began to socialise and date once more, wanting her life to take shape. She met Tom Buchanan in the spring and wrote to Gatsby.

Gatsby tells Nick that he does not think that Daisy ever loved Tom. He says she did not really know what she was saying the previous afternoon.

When Gatsby returned from France he went to Louisville while Daisy and Tom were still on their wedding trip. He wandered through the place where he had known Daisy.

After breakfast, Nick is reluctant to leave Gatsby. Before he goes, he tells him that he is better than all the others.

Jordan is annoyed with Nick when she calls him that afternoon, but he does not want to meet her just then. He tries, unsuccessfully, to call Gatsby.

The night before, George Wilson's friend Michaelis sat with him through the night. George mentioned Myrtle coming from the city a few months back with a bruised face. He also produced her dog leash. He told Michaelis that he could find out who killed her.

George thinks that Myrtle has been killed by her lover.

The next day, George makes his way on foot to West Egg to find Gatsby, the owner of the yellow car that killed his wife.

Gatsby is in his pool. His chauffeur hears the shots. Later, Nick arrives and discovers Gatsby's body. Wilson's body lies a little way off, in the grass.

Questions

1. Describe the atmosphere as this chapter begins.
   Use examples to illustrate your ideas.

2. What is stopping Gatsby from leaving town?

3. Why did Gatsby find Daisy "excitingly desirable"?
   What insight does this give you into Gatsby's character?

4. Are you surprised to discover that Daisy slept with Gatsby
   when she first knew him, five years ago?

5. Why did Gatsby feel married to Daisy?
   What is your response to this?

6. In your view, what attracted Gatsby to Daisy?

7. Describe Gatsby and Daisy on their last afternoon before
   he went abroad.
   Do you think they were in love?

8. Why didn't Daisy wait for Gatsby?
   What is your response to this?

9. "The letter reached Gatsby while he was still at Oxford."
   How must Gatsby have felt when he received this letter
   from Daisy?

10. Gatsby insists to Nick that Daisy never loved Tom.
    What makes him so insistent, do you think?

11.   What made Gatsby visit Louisville when he returned
      from France?
      Did he find what he was looking for, do you think?

12.   Is Gatsby idealistic and romantic in your view?

13.   Describe the atmosphere as Nick says goodbye to Gatsby.
      Why does he compliment his neighbour?

14.   How does Nick react to Jordan's phonecall?
      Can you explain his behaviour here?
      How would you feel if you were Jordan?

15.   What details about Myrtle does George mention to
      Michaelis?
      What is George doing at this point?

16.   'He murdered her.'
      What has happened to Myrtle, according to George?

17.   What does George do when Michaelis leaves him?

18.   How does the author describe what happens to Gatsby?
      Are you surprised by this turn of events?

19.   How do you feel when reading of Gatsby's murder?

20.   What does Nick mean when he says that Gatsby "must
      have felt that he had lost the old warm world"?

21.   Describe the mood as the chapter ends.

22.   Is this a fitting end for Gatsby?
        Explain your personal response.

Chapter Nine

Summary

Nightmare newspaper reports circulate the next morning.

Catherine, Myrtle's sister, stops the truth about the affair from coming out. She insists that Myrtle did not know Gatsby and that she was very happy with her husband.

Nick finds himself dealing with Gatsby's affairs alone. He calls Daisy, but she and Tom have left town, leaving no forwarding address.

He tries to contact Meyer Wolfsheim, but cannot get hold of him. Wolfsheim sends a letter, saying that he cannot come down to West Egg.

Nick answers a long distance phonecall from Chicago, thinking that it must be Daisy. The caller says someone is in trouble, that they have been picked up by the police. When Nick interrupts to say that he is not Gatsby, that Gatsby is dead, the call is disconnected.

Nick has difficulty locating any friends of Gatsby's.

Gatsby's father, Henry C. Gatz, comes for the funeral.

Nick goes to New York on the morning of the funeral, looking for Meyer Wolfsheim. Initially Wolfsheim will not see him, but when he does, he speaks highly of Gatsby. However, he refuses to attend the funeral.

Gatsby's father is full of pride for his son as he speaks to Nick. He feels that 'Jimmy' was bound to get ahead.

No mourners arrive for Gatsby's funeral, except the man with owl-eyed glasses from Gatsby's library, three months earlier.

Nick remembers travelling back West from school for Christmas. As a Westerner, Nick feels that the East has always been distorted for him, and more so after Gatsby's death. He decides to go home.

Before leaving, Nick meets with Jordan Baker, to leave things in order. She tells him she is already engaged to another man, which he doubts.

In October, Nick runs into Tom. He refuses to shake Tom's hand and asks him what he said to Wilson on the afternoon that Gatsby died.
Tom says that he told him who owned the car, and adds that Gatsby had it coming to him.

Nick spends his Saturday nights in New York, avoiding Gatsby's empty mansion that has been home to so many dazzling parties.

On his last night, Nick goes to look at Gatsby's house and sprawls on the beach. He imagines the Sound as it must have looked to the Dutch sailors who arrived there and saw a fresh new world.

He thinks of Gatsby's wonder when he first spotted the light of Daisy's dock and the man's optimism for the future.

Questions

1. Describe the scene at Gatsby's.

2. What is sensational and shocking about what has taken place?

3. What stops the whole story about Myrtle Wilson from coming out into the open?

4. "I found myself on Gatsby's side, and alone."
   What is going on here?

5. Why can't Nick reach Daisy by telephone?
   What is going on here?
   What is your reaction to this?

6. What is stopping Meyer Wolfsheim from coming to Gatsby's, in your view?

7. What does the long distance call from Chicago reveal?

8. How would you be feeling at this point, if you were Nick?

9. Describe Gatsby's father, Henry C. Gatz.

10. What view does Gatsby's father have of his son?
    Does this surprise you at all?

11. Why does Nick hang up on Klipspringer?

12. Are you surprised that Nick is struggling to find friends of Gatsby's?

13. How is Nick received when he goes to find Meyer Wolfsheim?
    Why is this, do you think?

14. Why won't Wolfsheim attend Gatsby's funeral?
    What is your response to this?

15. How do you respond to Henry C. Gatz's pride in his son?

16. Describe Gatsby's funeral.
    What is the mood like at this point?

17. Nobody comes to Gatsby's funeral.
    Why is this the case?
    How does this make you feel?
    Does this reveal anything to you about Jay Gatsby?

18. Why does Nick struggle to think about Gatsby at Gatsby's grave?

19. Owl Eyes calls Gatsby a "poor son-of-a-bitch."
    What makes him say this?

20. What is Nick's "Middle West"?
    Comment on the imagery here.

21. What makes Nick decide to go back West?

22. How do things end with Jordan?
    How does Nick feel about breaking up with her?

23.   When he sees him on Fifth Avenue, Nick asks Tom what
      he said to Wilson on the afternoon of Gatsby's death.
      What did Tom do here?
      What is your reponse to this?
      What would you have done in Tom's position?

24.   Why does Nick think that Tom and Daisy are careless
      people?

25.   Why does Nick spend his Saturday nights in New York?

26.   How does Gatsby's empty mansion contribute to the
      mood at this point?

27.   As the novel ends, do you think that Nick understands
      Gatsby?

28.   What is the mood like as the story closes?
      Explain your point of view fully.

29.   Do you like this ending?
      Give a reason for your answer.

Further Questions

1. Did you enjoy the ending of this novel?
    Why/why not?
    Is it a fitting ending for the story?
    What questions are you left with?

2. Comment on the imagery and descriptive language of the final section.

3. Does this story teach us anything about people?
    Does it teach us anything about life?
    Refer to the text to support the points you make.

4. How are the lives of the wealthy and privileged presented in this text?

5. What does this novel suggest about appearances and reality?

6. Do you think that the rich and famous of today lead lives similar to Gatsby and the Buchanans, or have things changed?

7. Is Nick a good narrator?
    Do you like how this story is told?

8.   Who is your favourite character in this novel?
       What do you like about them?

9.   Who is your least favourite character in this novel?
       What do you dislike about them?

10.   What are the major themes and issues in this text?
       How are they explored?
       What conclusions do you draw?

11.   What did you enjoy about this story?

12.   What did you dislike about this story?

13.   Is this novel engaging and entertaining?
       Explain your point of view.

14.   Does this novel remind you of any other novels you have
       read, or films you have seen? Explain your point of view,
       including examples.

Theme/Issue (HL)/Relationships (OL)

Relationships has been selected as the theme/issue to explore in relation to this text.

The theme of relationships can be applied to any relationship in a text and includes love, marriage, friendship and family bonds. Consider the complexities of relationships and the impact they have on characters' lives.

1. Does the speaker, Nick Carraway have a good relationship with his family?
   Use examples to support your point of view.

2. What view of Gatsby does Nick have as the novel begins?
   Does his view of him change throughout the novel?
   How does he view him as the story ends?
   Do they have a good relationship?
   How well do Nick and Gatsby communicate, interact and understand one another?
   Do Nick and Gatsby value each other's friendship?
   Are Nick and Gatsby honest with one another?
   Use examples to explain your view.

3. Does Nick have a good relationship with Daisy and Tom?
   In what ways do his relationships with Daisy and Tom change during the novel?

4.   Do Daisy and her husband, Tom, have a good
      relationship?
      Do they communicate well?
      Are they loving towards one another?
      Do they value one another?
      What does their infidelity suggest about their
      relationship?
      What weaknesses do you see in their relationship?
      What strengths do you see in their relationship?
      Does their relationship change over the course of the
      novel? Explain, using examples from the text.

5.   Do Tom and Myrtle (Mrs Wilson) have a good
      relationship?
      What is the effect of this affair on Tom's marriage?

6.   Do characters in this text truly love their partners?
      Use examples to explain your stance.

7.   What are your first impressions of Gatsby's re-union with
      Daisy?
      Do they love one another, do you think?

8.   Gatsby and Daisy's affair does not destroy her marriage.
      Why is this the case?
      What does this reveal about her relationship with Tom?

9.   At the end of Chapter Seven, Nick sees Tom and
      Daisy through their pantry window and they look as if
      they are "conspiring together".
      What does this suggest to you about their relationship?

10.   Does Gatsby love Daisy more than Tom does?
     Support your point of view with reference to the text.

11.   Does Daisy care who loves her most?
     What are her priorities, do you think?

12.   In Chapter Eight, we learn of the origins of Daisy and
     Gatsby's relationship.
     What does their history add to the theme of relationships
     in this novel?

13.   Why is it important to Gatsby that Daisy never loved
     Tom?
     What does this suggest about Gatsby's relationship with
     Daisy?

14.   What does Nick and Jordan's break-up in Chapter Nine
     reveal to you about their relationship?
     Do they really care about each other, in your view?
     Does Gatsby truly know and understand love? Why/why
     not?

15.   Do characters in this text have a realistic view of love?
     Explain, using examples from the text to support the
     points that you make.

16.   What is the most significant relationship in this story?
     What makes this relationship stand out for you?
     What does it tell us about human relationships, friendship
     and love?

17.   Are relationships in this story positive or negative?
      Are they meaningful or shallow?
      What makes them this way?

18.   Are a lot of the relationships in this novel characterised by
      conflict?
      Explain your point of view.

19.   What else characterises relationships in this text? (Are
      they generally supportive, secretive, honest, loving, etc.?)

20.   Do relationships in this story bring characters happiness
      or sorrow?
      Include examples in your answer.

21.   What makes relationships difficult in this text?

22.   What helps relationships in this text?

23.   How do relationships change during the story?

24.   What do you learn about relationships from reading this
      novel?

25.   Are relationships portrayed realistically in this text?
      Make use of examples to support the points that you
      make.

26.   Are relationships in this story interesting and involving?
      Explain your point of view, using examples to illustrate
      your ideas.

27.   Does any aspect of the theme of relationships in this text shock, upset or unsettle you?

Use examples to help explain your point of view.

Cultural Context (HL)/Social Setting (OL)

Cultural Context/Social Setting refers to the world of the text.
Consider social norms, beliefs, values and attitudes.

1.   How do you know that the narrator, Nick Carraway, is privileged and wealthy?

2.   How do the descriptions of West Egg in Chapter One add to your understanding of where this story is set?

3.   When he first goes to Tom and Daisy's, the speaker describes them as old friends he scarcely knows. Does this comment reveal anything to you about this world?

4.   What does Tom's attitude to race reveal to you about his values and attitudes?

5.   What does Tom's having a woman in New York tell you about his attitude to women and marriage?

6.   What does Daisy's attitude to her daughter reveal about this world?

7.   In Chapter One, Tom and Daisy believed Nick to be engaged, as they had heard rumours to this effect.
      What do these rumours and gossip reveal about this world?
      What does the fact that this topic was not mentioned until the end of the evening tell you about this world?

8.   What does the lifestyle of Daisy and Tom Buchanan indicate about this world?

9.   What does the party in Myrtle's apartment reveal to you about these people?
      Note each observation that you make.

10.   At Mrs Wilson's party, her sister remarks that she almost made the mistake of marrying beneath her.
      What do Catherine's sentiments reveal about the values and attitudes of her world?

11.   Tom strikes Myrtle and breaks her nose at the party in the apartment.
      What is your reaction to this?
      What does this tell you about Tom and the society of the novel?

12.   Chapter Three begins with a description of Gatsby's elaborate parties.
      What insight do these parties give you into Gatsby's society and his place in it?

13.   Gatsby's parties are very lavish and his guests are very rich.

Do they enjoy these gatherings?

Why do so many univited guests come each week?

14. Why does Gatsby stage these parties?

What does he get out of them?

15. How does Tom Buchanan's history of infidelity contribute to your view of this world?

16. Why does Gatsby want Daisy to see his home and grounds?

What does this suggest about attitudes and values in this world?

17. Does the fact that Gatsby changed his name and re-invented himself tell you anything about this world?

18. In Chapter Six Tom Buchanan says that, "...women run around too much these days to suit me. They meet all kinds of crazy fish."

Comment on his attitude here.

19. In Chapter Seven, Daisy's daughter is brought in by the nurse to meet her mother's guests.

What does this episode reveal to you about this world?

20. In Chapter Seven Tom remarks that, "next they'll throw everything overboard and have intermarriage between black and white."

What does this comment reveal about his attitude?

21.   Tom reveals that Gatsby is involved in bootlegging and worse.
        How does this affect the esteem the others hold him in?
        Why is this the case?
        Is his wealth not enough to earn him respectability?

22.   "...he took Daisy one still October night, took her because he had no real right to touch her hand..."
        How does this detail from Gatsby's past (Chapter Eight) add to your understanding of this world?

23.   Nobody attends Gatsby's funeral.
        What does this tell you about his friends, associates and party guests?

24.   In a way, Gatsby pays for his affair with Daisy with his life.
        Is this fair?
        What does this suggest about this world?

25.   Daisy and Tom leave town to avoid the consequences of Mrs Wilson's accident.
        Why are they able to do this?

26.   Why do Gatsby's friends 'vanish' following his death?
        What does this reveal to you about these people?

27.   What is the significance of World War One in the characters' lives?

28.   Is Gatsby's world both reality and fantasy, fact and fiction? Explain, referring to the text to support your answer.

29.   What time and place is this story set in?

30.   Is this world a romantic or practical place? Explain your point of view.

31.   Are wealth and class important in this world? What view do characters have towards money and class?

32.   Is race important in this world?

33.   Are characters in this text moral and upstanding?

34.   What do characters value in this story?

35.   What kind of society do you see in this text? (How do people treat one another? What do they believe in? What is important to them?)

36.   Is there violence and conflict in this world? Where do you see this violence and conflict?

37.   Is this a secure or dangerous world?

38.   What is the role of women in the world of this novel?

39.   How are women viewed and treated in this story?

40.   Is family important in the world of this text?

41. What is the most important thing to characters in this world?
What is your response to this?

42. Are characters in this world free to live as they choose, or must they conform to society's expectations?

43. Is this world a supportive or destructive environment for the novel's characters?

44. Is the world of this text a magical or mysterious place?
Use examples to justify your viewpoint.

45. Would you like to live in the world of 'The Great Gatsby'?
Include examples to justify your viewpoint.

46. Are friendship and love important in this world, or are characters self-centred and self-serving?
Justify your viewpoint with reference to the text.

47. Is their world a warm, loving place, or a cold, unfeeling place?
Justify your viewpoint with reference to the text.

Literary Genre (HL)

Literary Genre refers to the way the story is told. Consider aspects of narration such as the manner and style of narration, characterisation, setting, tension, literary techniques, etc.

1. This novel is told in the first person, from the point of view of Nick Carraway.
    What is the effect of this on the storytelling?

2. Is Nick a reliable narrator?
    Explain your point of view.

3. How does the narrator spark our curiosity about Gatsby as the novel begins?
    How is this curiosity maintained throughout the tale?

4. Comment on the language and style of the novel.
    Do you enjoy how it is written?

5. Does a lot happen in the opening chapter?
    What is the purpose of this opening chapter?

6. What does Tom's woman in New York add to the story?

7. How does the party in Mrs Wilson's apartment contribute to the atmosphere of the story? (Chapter Two)
    What does this party reveal to you about these characters?

8.   Does the author present Tom and his mistress as a happy couple?
Use examples to support the points you make.

9.   How does the author develop and maintain a sense of mystery and intrigue surrounding Jay Gatsby throughout the novel?
What does this mysterious quality add to the novel?

10.   How is a surreal atmosphere created in Chapter Three?
What is the effect of creating this feeling in the reader?

11.   In Chapter Six we learn that Gatsby is really James Gatz, that he re-invented himself at seventeen.
How does this add to your understanding of his character?

12.   Comment on the atmosphere and mood of Gatsby's parties.
What does this add to the novel?

13.   What makes the scene in the Plaza Hotel in Chapter Seven so tense?
Consider tension as a literary device here.

14.   What does Myrtle's death add to the story?
Is this an unexpected twist?

15.   In Chapter Eight, what does the account of Gatsby and Daisy's past add to the story?

16.   What is your reaction to the manner of Gatsby's death?
Is his death described in violent terms?

Why, do you think, does the author choose to describe it this way?

Is this a sad event in the novel? Explain your view.

17. What does Nick learn about Gatsby after his death?

How does this add to your understanding of the novel?

18. Do we ever really know Gatsby?

Refer to the text to support your viewpoint.

19. Does this novel have a satisfying ending?

Explain your point of view.

20. Comment on the mood as the story ends.

21. Is Gatsby the story's hero? Is Nick?

Explain your choice fully.

22. What makes Gatsby an interesting and memorable character?

23. Does the reader always know exactly what is going on in this novel?

Explain your viewpoint.

How does the author achieve this?

What is the effect of this?

24. How does setting contribute to the story?

How does the setting of Gatsby's mansion add to the story?

25.   Do you find this novel to be interesting and easy to read?
Include examples in your answer.

26.   What makes Jay Gatsby a complex character?
Is he an attractive or repellent character?
Include specific details in your answer.

27.   Is Tom an interesting and complex character?
Is he an attractive or repellent character?
Include specific details in your answer.

28.   Do you enjoy the role that coincidence plays in the story?

29.   What draws the reader into this story?
Highlight specific aspects of the text in your answer.

30.   How does the author create a dark, sinister edge to the story at times?

31.   How do weather and the seasons contribute to the storytelling of this narrative?

32.   Identify the various sources of conflict in this text.
How does conflict add to the story?

33.   Does the author create the sensation that the reader has learned and developed from their time with Gatsby, just as Nick has?
If so, how has he done this?

34. What are the high points of this novel?
    What makes them exciting and intriguing?

35. Did you enjoy the storyline of the text?
    Was it exciting, compelling, tense or emotional?
    Use examples from the text to support your answer.

36. Is there just one plot or many plots?
    What connections can you make between these
    storylines?

37. What interested you most in the story?

38. Are characters vivid, realistic and well-developed?
    Explain your point of view, using examples from the text.

39. Who is your favourite character in this novel?
    What makes you like/admire them?

40. Who is your least favourite character in this novel?
    What makes you dislike them?

41. Do you empathise or identify with any characters?

42. What themes can you identify in this story?

43. Does this novel have an elusive, surreal, dream-like ,
    quality to it?
    If so, how is this achieved?
    What does this add to the story?

44. Is this a tragic tale?

45.   How does the author create suspense, high emotion and excitement in this text?

What techniques does he use to good advantage?

46.   Consider the author's use of tension and resolution in the novel.

What are the major tensions/problems/conflicts in the text?

Are they resolved or not?

47.   Does the author make use of any striking patterns of imagery or symbols to add to this story?

48.   How does the aythor make use of the unexpected?

What does this add to the story?

49.   What is the climax (high point) of the story?

What do you think of this moment?

How does it make you feel?

50.   Comment on the language of the novel.

How does dialogue add to the story?

51.   What do you find moving or emotional in this novel?

52.   What aspects of the novel form worked well in this story, in your view?

53.   What do you like about the way this story is told?

54.   To what genre does this novel belong?

Support your choice with examples from the text.

55.   *The Great Gatsby* is considered by many to be the "Great American Novel." Why is this the case, do you think?

General Vision and Viewpoint (HL)

General Vision and Viewpoint refers to the author's outlook or view of life and how this viewpoint is represented in the text.

1. How does it being summer and the speaker making plans contribute to the outlook of the opening chapter?

2. How does Tom's woman in New York affect the atmosphere of the opening chapter?
   What does this suggest about his life?
   What does this suggest about his marriage?
   Does it darken or brighten the mood of this opening chapter?
   Explain your reasons fully.

3. Has their wealth made Tom and Daisy happy?
   Why/why not? What makes you say this?

4. In Chapter Two, the guests at Myrtle Wilson's party seem rather bored.
   Why are these characters bored?
   What does this suggest about life?

5. 'Neither of them can stand the person they're married to.'
   What does Tom and Myrtle's (Mrs Wilson's) relationship suggest about life in this text?
   What does it suggest about love?

6.   The people attending Mrs Wilson's party are all very
      wealthy.
      Are they happy and content with life?
      Include examples in your answer.

7.   How does the reunion of Gatsby and Daisy contribute to
      the story's outlook?
      Is their romance full of possibility?

8.   Gatsby is very keen for Daisy to see his mansion.
      Why is this the case?
      What does this suggest about what is important in life?
      How does this make you feel?

9.   What do Gatsby's spectacular parties reveal to you about
      life?

10.   How has Gatsby earned his wealth?
      How does this affect the General Vision and Viewpoint of
      the text?

11.   What details about the Buchanans suggest that they are
      adrift or purposeless?

12.   What does Myrtle Wilson's accidental death suggest
      about life?

13.   What does Gatsby's death reveal about the author's
      attitude to life?
      Is this a positive or negative outlook?

14.   What sort of life does Gatsby have?

       Is this a positive or negative portrayal of life and living?

15.   Even before Gatsby's death, it appears that Daisy has decided to stay with Tom.

       How does Daisy's choice impact on the General Vision and Viewpoint of this text?

16.   Is there a certain magic to Gatsby's lifestyle, however fleeting and elusive it may be?

17.   Following Gatsby's death, his friends disappear.

       How does this make you feel?

       What does this suggest about life?

18.   Are characters in this text hopeful and forward looking about life?

       Are they realistic? Do they make well-thought out plans?

       What does this suggest about their outlook on life?

19.   What comments do characters make on their society and the problems they are facing?

20.   Are characters happy or unhappy?

21.   What makes characters in this story happy and fulfilled?

22.   What makes characters in this story unhappy and unfulfilled?

23.   Are relationships destructive or nurturing?
        What do they reveal about life as we see characters
        supported/thwarted in their efforts to grow/mature?

24.   Is life full of possibility and potential in this text?

25.   Are imagery and language bright or dark in the text?
        (Tone of the text)

26.   What is the mood of this text?
        Include examples to justify your ideas.

27.   Does this novel suggest that life is magical or vacuous?
        Support your points with reference to the text.

28.   What does this novel suggest about human nature?
        Is this outlook positive or negative?

29.   Do characters face many obstacles and difficulties in this
        text? Do they struggle?
        Why/why not?

30.   Is this text dark and bleak or uplifting and inspiring?
        Give reasons for your view.

31.   Is there a lesson or moral to this story?
        What could it be?
        Does it still hold true today?

32.   What does this story teach us about life?

33.   How do you feel as you read the novel?
        Refer to key moments to anchor your answer.

34. Does the novel end on a hopeful, optimistic note, or
    a hopeless, pessimistic one?
    Are questions raised by the text resolved by the end?
    Are they resolved happily or unhappily?
    How do you feel at the end?
    Explain your point of view.

35. Are you hopeful or despairing regarding the prospects for
    human happiness in this story?
    (Are characters likely to be happy?)

36. Identify the aspects of life that the author concentrates on.
    Are they positive or negative?
    What is he telling us by focusing on these aspects of life?

37. Identify bright, hopeful, optimistic aspects of the novel.

38. Identify dark, hopeless, pessimistic aspects of the novel.

39. Does this novel offer a comforting or disturbing view of
    life?
    Overall, is it optimistic or pessimistic?
    Explain your point of view.

Hero, Heroine, Villain (OL)

'Hero, Heroine, Villain' refers to central characters (protagonists/antagonists).

Their traits, values, etc. and their ability to deal with conflict, challenges, obstacles, etc. should be considered.

Gatsby

1. What strengths do you see in Gatsby's character?

2. What weaknesses do you see in Gatsby's character?

3. How much do we know about the source of Gatsby's wealth?
    How does this affect your view of him?

4. Does Gatsby love Daisy?
    Is he a romantic figure?

5. Gatsby does not turn Daisy over to the police when she knocks Myrtle down and kills her.
    Is this noble of him? Explain your view.

6. Gatsby reinvented himself when he was seventeen, even giving himself a new name.
What does this tell you about the man?

7. What gives Gatsby an air of mystery?

8. Is Gatsby an authentic character, or is he a faker?

9. What makes Gatsby thrive in the world of this novel?

10. Is Gatsby materialistic and superficial, in your view?

11. What does Gatsby value?

12. How well does Gatsby cope with conflict?

13. How well does Gatsby cope with obstacles/challenges?

14. Do we ever *really* know Gatsby?
Support your view with reference to the novel.

15. Is Gatsby a happy and content character?
Explain your viewpoint fully.

16. What makes Gatsby an interesting character in your opinion?

17. If you could chat to Gatsby, what would you talk about?
What advice would you give him?
What questions would you ask?

Tom Buchanan

1.   What strengths do you see in Tom's character?

2.   What weaknesses do you see in Tom's character?

3.   Does Tom love Daisy?
        Is he a romantic figure?

4.   What do Tom's many affairs with women suggest about
        him?

5.   Is Tom an arrogant man?

6.   Is Tom full of passion and feeling?

7.   What does Tom value?

8.   How well does Tom cope with conflict?

9.   How well does Tom cope with obstacles/challenges?

10.   Is Tom a happy and content character?
        Explain your viewpoint fully.

11.   What makes Tom an interesting character in your
        opinion?

12.   If you could chat to Tom, what would you talk about?
        What advice would you give him?
        What questions would you ask?

The Comparative Study: Comparing Texts

Use the following questions to compare your texts, noting the similarities and differences between them. Include examples to support the points that you make.

Theme/Issue - Relationships

1.   Are relationships in this text more positive and supportive than the relationships in your other chosen texts?
     Include specific examples in your answer.

2.   Rank the relationships you have studied in your various texts from most positive (score of 10) to most negative (score of 1).
     Add a note explaining your choices.

3.   Are relationships in this text the most engaging and interesting that you have studied?
     Explain your choice.

4.   Rank the relationships you have studied in your various texts from the most interesting (score of 10) to the least interesting (score of 1).
Add a note explaining your choices.

5.   Did you learn most about the theme of relationships from this text or another text on your Comparative Study course?
Refer to your chosen texts to support your answer.

6.   What similarities do you notice in the theme of relationships in this text and your other Comparative Study texts?

7.   What differences do you notice in the theme of relationships in this text and your other Comparative Study texts?

8.   How do the events of the text impact on the characters' relationships with one another in this text and your other chosen texts?
Who is most affected?
Who is least affected?

9.   How does conflict impact on the relationships of characters in this text and your other chosen texts?
Who is most affected?
Who is least affected?

10.   How does social class impact on the relationships of characters in this text and your other chosen texts?

Who is most affected?

Who is least affected?

11.   Is the theme of relationships portrayed in an idealistic or realistic way in each of your chosen texts?

12.   Did any aspect of the theme of relationships shock or surprise you in your three chosen texts?
Use examples from your texts to support the points that you make.

13.   What are the most interesting aspects of the theme of relationships in each of your chosen texts?

14.   Which text taught you most about relationships?
Refer to each text in your answer.

15.   What key moments best capture the theme of relationships in each of your texts?

16.   What similarities do you notice in the theme of relationships in this text and your other comparative study texts?

17.   What differences do you notice in the theme of relationships in this text and your other comparative study texts?

Literary Genre

1.   Did you like the way this story was told more than your other comparative texts?
State what you enjoyed most (and least) about each.

2.   Is this text more exciting than your other texts?
Consider tension, suspense, pacing, conflict and the author's use of the unexpected.

3.   How does the author make use of tension in each of your chosen texts?
Where is it most effective?
Where is it least effective?
Use examples to support your point of view.

4.   How does the author make use of climax in each of your chosen texts?
Where is it most effective?
Where is it least effective?
Use examples to support your point of view.

5.   How does the author make use of resolution in each of your chosen texts?
Where is it most effective?
Where is it least effective?
Use examples to support your point of view.

6. Are characters more engaging in this text than in your other texts?
Refer to each of your texts in your answer.

7. How does the author create vivid, memorable characters in each of your chosen texts?

8. In which of your texts are characters most life-like and compelling?
In which text are characters least life-like and difficult to relate to?
Refer to each of your texts in your answer.

9. Is the setting more effective in telling the story in this text, than in your other texts?

10. Is setting more central to the story in this text or another text you have studied as part of your Comparative Study?

11. Is this text more unpredictable than your other texts?
Refer to each of your texts in your answer.

12. Does this text have greater emotional power than your other texts?
Was this emotional power created in a more interesting way here or in a different text?
Refer to each of your texts in your answer.

13. What was your favourite literary technique, used by the author of each of your texts?
How did the use of this technique help the storytelling?

14. To what extent are you influenced by the point of view that this story is told from?
Are you influenced to a greater or lesser degree by the point of view utilised in your other Comparative Study texts?

15. What key moments best capture Literary Genre in each of your texts?

16. What similarities do you notice in the Literary Genre of this text and your other Comparative Study texts?
Mention specific aspects of narrative.

17. What differences do you notice in the Literary Genre of this text and your other Comparative Study texts?
Mention specific aspects of narrative.

General Vision and Viewpoint

1. Is life happier and fuller for characters in this text than in your other Comparative Study texts?
Explain your point of view fully.

2. Do characters in this text face more obstacles and difficulties than in your other texts?
Who struggles most?

3. Are characters in this text rewarded more for their struggles than in your other texts?

Do they overcome adversity and achieve true happiness and contentment in a way that is not realised in your other texts?

4.   How do events in these texts, and your personal response to these events, help your understanding of the General Vision and Viewpoint of these texts?
Include specific examples in your answer.

5.   How does your attitude to central characters help shape your understanding of the General Vision and Viewpoint of your chosen texts?
Include specific reference to your chosen characters in your answer.

6.   What aspects of this text did you respond to emotionally? How does this help your understanding of the General Vision and Viewpoint of the text?
How does this compare to your other texts?

7.   Is this the brightest, most hopeful and triumphant text you have studied?
Explain why its message is more or less positive than in your other texts.

8.   Which of your chosen texts was the bleakest and most upsetting or depressing?
Explain what made it more negative than your other texts. What made them more positive?

9.   Plot your three texts on a scale of one to ten from darkest (most pessimistic) to brightest (most optimistic). Add a note to explain their positions.

10.   What key moments best capture the General Vision and Viewpoint of each of your texts?

11.   What similarities do you notice in the General Vision and Viewpoint of this text and your other Comparative Study texts?

12.   What differences do you notice in the General Vision and Viewpoint of this text and your other Comparative Study texts?

13.   Can you relate any aspect of this text to your own life experience?
        If so, how does this help to shape your understanding of the General Vision and Viewpoint of this text?

Cultural Context/Social Setting

Consider each of your chosen texts in your answers.

1.   In which of the texts you have studied for the Comparative Study do characters have the most freedom and choice?
        Justify your answer with examples from your chosen texts.

2. In which of your texts are characters most controlled?

3. Who holds the power in each world?
   Who is powerless?

4. In which of your texts do characters have the most freedom?
   Why is this the case?

5. In which world is difference most accepted and respected?
   In which world is difference least accepted and respected?

6. Which world is the least tolerant?
   Which world is the most tolerant?
   Include examples to explain your view.

7. Which world is the best to live in if you are a woman?
   Give reasons for your answer.

8. Which world is the best to live in if you are a man?
   Give reasons for your answer.

9. Which world is the best to live in if you are a child?
   Give reasons for your answer.

10. Which text portrays the most violent and volatile world?

11. Which of your texts portrays the safest, most secure place?

12. Which of your texts portrays the most supportive world?

13. Which of these worlds is the darkest, most fearful place?

14.   Which of these worlds is the brightest, most joyful place?

15.   Which of these places is the most unpredictable?

16.   Which text portrays the most traditional world?

17.   Which of these societies holds family in the highest esteem?

18.   Which of these societies holds love in the highest esteem? Which of these societies holds love in the lowest esteem?

19.   Which of these societies holds religion in the highest esteem?
      Which of these societies holds religion in the lowest esteem?

20.   Which of these societies holds power in the highest esteem?

21.   Which of these societies holds wealth in the highest esteem?

22.   Where do you see the best treatment of the vulnerable of society? Include examples to support your view.

23.   Where do you see the worst treatment of the vulnerable of society? Include examples to support your view.

24.   Which of the worlds you have studied is the most materialistic?
      Which of the worlds you have studied is the least

materialistic?

What makes characters have these outlooks?

25. Which of the worlds you have studied is the most secretive?

What makes characters behave this way?

26. Which of your texts displays the greediest world?

What makes characters have this attitude?

27. Where is love most important?

Where is love most successful?

Where is love least important?

Where is love least succesful?

Compare the success of love in each of your chosen texts.

What does this tell you about the worlds of these texts and characters' lives?

28. Which of these worlds appealed to you most?

Give reasons for your answer.

29. Which of these worlds appealed to you least?

Explain your point of view.

30. Which of your texts is home to the most religious or spiritual world?

31. Which of your texts showed the least religious or spiritual society?

32. How important is social class in each of your texts?

33. In which of your texts are characters most accepting of their world and society?

34. In which of your texts do characters challenge their world, society and values most?

35. In which of your texts do you see the greatest inequality?

36. In which of your texts do you see the greatest injustice?

37. Where do characters behave the best towards one another?
How does Cultural Context/Social Setting influence their behaviour?

38. How do characters reflect the Cultural Context/Social Setting of their worlds?
Explain, including examples.

39. How does the Cultural Context/Social Setting of your texts lead to problems and difficulties for the texts' characters?
How does it affect characters' responses to these difficulties?

40. What key moments best capture the Cultural Context/ Social Setting of each of your texts?

41. What similarities do you notice in the Cultural Context/ Social Setting of this text and your other Comparative Study texts?

42. What differences do you notice in the Cultural Context/ Social Setting of this text and your other Comparative Study texts?

Hero/Heroine/Villain

Consider the following list of questions for a central character in each of your chosen texts.

1. Who is the most interesting character in the text?
   What makes them interesting?
   What do you like about them?
   What do you dislike about them?
   What are this character's strengths?
   What are this character's weaknesses?

2. How does this character cope with conflict?

3. How does this character cope with the unexpected?

4. Are they a resourceful character?

5. Are they an emotional character?
   Use examples to support your view.

6. Do you empathise with this character? Why/why not?

7. What do you admire about this character?

8. How well does this character relate to and interact with other characters?

   Include examples to support your points.

9. Is this character happy or sad?

10. Are they an active or passive character?

    How do they contribute to the action and storyline of the text?

    Are they important to the story's plot and development?

11. Is this character a good (successful and interesting) main character?

12. Would you like to meet this character?

    If you met them, what would you talk about?

13. If you had any advice for this character, what would it be?

14. Does this character make the story more exciting?

    In what way do they do this?

15. Is this character a hero/heroine or a villain?

    Explain your choice.

16. Identify the key moments in the text that illustrate your chosen character's personality traits/character.

17. On a scale of one to ten (with one being extremely heroic and ten being an evil villain), where would you place your chosen character?

    Give reasons for your choice.

Where would you place the main characters from your other texts?

Why would you place them here?

18. Which of your chosen characters do you like and admire most?

What makes them your favourite character?

Give reasons for your answer.

19. Which of your chosen characters do you dislike most?

Explain why you like some more than others.

20. Which of your chosen characters shocked you most?

Give reasons for your answer.

21. Which of your chosen characters impressed you most?

Give reasons for your answer.

22. Which of your chosen characters did you feel most sorry for?

Give reasons for your answer.

23. Who is the most resourceful character you have come across?

Give reasons for your answer.

24. Which of your chosen characters faced the most problems and difficulties?

Did they cope well with these problems?

25. How is your favourite character similar to the characters in your other texts?

26. How is your favourite character different to the characters in your other texts?

27. Choose key moments from each of your texts to highlight your characters' strengths and weaknesses.

CLASSROOM QUESTIONS GUIDES

Books of questions, designed to save teachers time and lead to rewarding classroom experiences.

www.SceneBySceneGuides.com

Lightning Source UK Ltd.
Milton Keynes UK
UKHW021952130120
356877UK00006B/560/P